AN IMMIGRANT'S GUIDE TO NAVIGATING BORDERS AND BODIES OF WATER

poems

An Immigrant's Guide to Navigating Borders and Bodies of Water

AILEEN CASSINETTO

PALOMA PRESS
San Mateo & Morgan Hill, California

Copyright © 2025 Aileen Cassinetto

ISBN: 9781734496567

Library of Congress Control Number: 2025946065

Book Design by C. Sophia Ibardaloza

Cover image was adapted and modified by the book designer from an illustration in *A New Universal Atlas of the World* (1825).

ALL RIGHTS RESERVED

No part of this publication may be reproduced, distributed, or transmitted in any form or by any means, including photocopying, recording, or other electronic or mechanical methods, without the prior written permission of the publisher, except in the case of brief quotations embodied in critical reviews and certain other noncommercial uses permitted by copyright law. For permission requests, contact: editor@palomapress.org

Published by Paloma Press
San Mateo & Morgan Hill, California
www.palomapress.org

Paloma Press is an award-winning independent literary press on the San Francisco Peninsula. Our mission is to publish poetry and other literary works that honor our shared histories and inspire our creative futures.

Printed in the United States of America

CONTENTS

Latitudes

Let Me Call You Sweetheart	11
Traje de Boda	15
Heritage Fruit	16
I Am, Villanelle	17
Viand	19
Orange Jessamine Road	20
Imagine	22
In the Island of Good Boots	24
False Memory	26
The Art of Salamat	28
Martial Law Babies	31
Balikbayan	32
To Want the Wide American Earth	33
Pagbabalik	34
Legacy	35
At the Convalescent Home for Winter Plums,	37
Dust	38
A Short History of Journey	39
An American Sentence	41

Longitudes

An Immigrant's Guide to Navigating Borders and Bodies of Water	45
Speak Poetry	47
What I Know About Jawns I Learned From Allen Iverson	48
Haint Blue	50
There are no kings in America	51
To Treasure Island for a wardrobe fitting before the funeral cortège in Season 4 of Man in the High Castle	53
The Oldest English-Speaking Settlement on the San Francisco Peninsula	55
Still, Like Air	56
How to Build a Life	59
Kiss Me Over the Garden Gate	60
Ai Is Love	61
Tree Lighting at Fremont Park in the Second Year of the Pandemic	62
Poetry, please	63
Here be dragons, cetaceans, pink crustaceans, dear humans & a book of remembrance	65
A Trade War in Full Bloom, or How to Unpack the Love Language of Perishables as Import Duties Wilt the Fragile Trade of Flowers	67
Take Heart	68

Fireborn	69
Field Notes from Cooley Landing	70
Catalog of Cures in Ordinary Time	71
In Half Moon Bay	73
Great Expectations at Race & Auzerais	74
Glossary	75
Mapping Migrations:	
A Personal & Incomplete History	77
Acknowledgments	83

LATITUDES

"Geography is the key, the crucial accident of birth."
—Annie Dillard

LET ME CALL YOU SWEETHEART

> "The power that rules the Pacific, therefore, is the power that rules the world. And with the Philippines, that power is and will forever be the American Republic."
> —Albert Jeremiah Beveridge, United States Senator (1899-1911)

Nobody asked what we wanted.
We were entangled in the fate of empires
as one falls and another rises.
And we stood ravaged, squatted like
our mothers over guava leaves
and steaming water, moist heat soothing
the perineal wound of childing.
Fruit and spice mix with blood, now clotting,
jelly-like and metallic. Sweetheart,
say *sinta*—the stress is on the second
syllable, almost like a serenade,
or a slight movement, susurrous
and so dear. *Let me hear you whisper*—
honey is thicker than blood is thicker

than water. What to make of the slaughter,
in a time of cholera just before
the St. Louis World's Fair where our kin
were made to put on a show of butchering
and eating dogs, twenty or more each week

in the name of empire—a baptism
of fire. How do you like your *dinuguan?*
Soupy and smooth and savory.
Our mothers' mothers made it with offal,
but the secret is in the pig's blood.
Add a little vinegar before cooking.
Add more when simmering but never boiling.
Keep the love-light glowing, keep the water
bubbling, then let it rest. Add guava leaves,

and honey, I'm talking about tea,
a remedy for cholera—
malady of war, a mastery
of paired movements like populations
and their afflictions. How much of might
is mettle? What is the measure of an age.
At Manila Bay, we buried
one empire and birthed another.
Before the century ended,
we were a colony twice over,
an archipelago of blood and ash.
What is the color of empire as it sits
on the Pacific, with all the might
of an age. Where lies its heart and undoing.

First order of business was to quash
the rebellion and impose English
as the language of chance and circumstance.
Mind your diction and maledictions.

The irony was that McKinley
didn't even want us, "could not have told
where [our] darned islands were within
2,000 miles." His words. But moral
obligation is a force that bests
the burdens of annexation,
as does having a foothold in Asia.
All told, hem-haw, McKinley could not let go:
"When I next realized the Philippines
had dropped into our laps I confess

I did not know what to do with them.
We could not give them back to Spain,
that would be cowardly and dishonorable;
we could not turn them over to France
and Germany, that would be bad business
and discreditable; we could not leave
them to themselves, they were unfit for self-
government." But one day, I promise you,
my people will board a ship, split the ocean,
walk on water, scorch the earth, lose
our continent, all to show how well
we speak in English, the kind no one wants
to hear. We have lost more than what is
bearable, devoted our days

to finding a habitable language,
to building a dwelling of seawater and ash.
How much of it is ours, how much to keep,

how much to let slip. *Let me call you sweetheart,*
let me find a way to start over, stay
closer, one island to another. Here lies
our heart and undoing. Say *sinta—*
shelter and shutter, sum of our struggles.
We are more than our history,
our manifest destiny. We are a love
story older than the sea. Sweetheart, ask me
what I want as I tread wildly, feel
the belly of green turtles and gentle giants,
citizens of the great Philippine Sea.

TRAJE DE BODA

For Sophie

I longed to
be beautiful,
outside

of you. See
me live
my

ironies. I will
drape exquisitely,
therefore,

be still. Let
us be
perfect

for a day,
and, thereafter,
depend

on incompleteness, which
begs for
beginnings.

HERITAGE FRUIT

A cento

To a nightmare of mad bees
near blossoming time has come,
wake the buried seeds.

They say this is the heart
the greenest nectarines,
all the cold, terrible sweethearts.

The spectrum of tint,
fruit of this America.
Odd monsters breed here,

claw at the same straws,
scale all love down,
they are almost flowers,

*blooming with teeth
in the final hour.*

---

[1] Eileen R. Tabios, [2] Marjorie Evasco, [3] Ivy Alvarez, [4] Barbara Jane Reyes, [5] Angela Narciso Torres, [6] Mookie Katigbak Lacuesta, [7] Dinah Roma, [8] Luisa A. Igloria, [9] Merlie Alunan, [10] Ophelia Dimalanta, [11] Edith Tiempo, [12] Conchitina Cruz

I AM, VILLANELLE

I am from *balikbayan* boxes, veiled markers of identity.
I am from sunken galleons, misspent fragment of empires.
I am from hand-knotted piña fibers, a cultivar of possibilities.

I am from blue and white pottery, ghostly and full of stories.
I am from unglazed earthenware, seasoned with intent and fire.
I am from *balikbayan* boxes, movement of tenacity.

I am from the heartwood of wounded lign aloes, an
    unfortunate luxury.
I am from Glory of the Sea Cone, prized for its venom and spire.
I am from ocean crossings, an arbitrary and seaworthy possibility.

I am from repeated prayers and offerings, a Hail Mary pass and
    nine days to mercy.
I am from ghosts with a grievance, manifesting ire and satire.
I am from a precarious bloodline, a *balikbayan* genealogy.

I am from the mother of all fiestas, sanguinary and
    exhibiting miraculously.
I am from broken rosaries, indulgence for wayward outliers.
I am from possibilities in a family tree that doesn't end with me.

I am from buried treaties north of an archipelago, debris
   of synchronicity.
I am from a chronology of losses, curving ever higher.
I am from *balikbayan* boxes, veiled markers of identity.
I am foreshadowed in good faith, a possibility, empire
   of sundries.

VIAND

> *is a barbarian from the North*
> *sitting on a pile of rice.*
> —Paul Cassinetto

At her chi- chi Manila school,
she was forbidden to ~~think~~ speak
in Pilipino. So at lunch time,
eager to share her "ulam",
she would ask, "What is your viand?"
"Viand?" her husband repeats.
"Viand," she says more emphatically.
"That was what we called the dishes
we ate with rice when I was in third grade."
"Viand," her husband laughs, not having
encountered the word before,
and on whom language was never forced
and, consequently, never wrested.
"It sounds more like a D&D character."

ORANGE JESSAMINE ROAD

in summertime, is a chalk-drawn
    hopscotch court. Every face evoked is young
        and wraithlike, springing forth, wildcrafted—

hibiscus, mock orange, lemon grass;
    breadnut and black plum; star apple,
        sweetsop, rose apple. You,

most beautiful and most brave, leapt boldly
    towards your moon, marked
        with the rind of a fruit and

the incidental leaf, silvery,
    from a golden leaf tree. But then, you were tangled
        mid-air, between a rosy expanse

and your half-circle on the ground. You landed,
    outwardly unfazed, on a chalk-drawn line.
        Yesterday, I thought of you.

How in the days of your invincibility, I was
    invincible, too, felled only
        by whiteflies and afternoon naps.

I wondered if you ever found
    that rind of fruit,
        if you remembered to jump,

over mock oranges,
    over star apples,
        over your moon.

IMAGINE

It is 1919, and I am older
than my great-grandmother, parturient

and silent, as her husband responds
to an unyielding desire to be free

and sovereign. Imagine a scene
where the rules apply to everything.

In 1919, she must have feared
influenza and her husband's

inconstancy more than any army
of colonists. Her past, my future,

relative and happening at once.
Swear not by the fickle moon, I tell her,

except when it covers the sun completely.
Imagine a scene, an astronomer

measuring the positions of stars
to prove a new theory of gravity.

Show me again how starlight bends
as it passes by the limb of the sun.

Like my great-grandmother bending under
the pressure that is her husband's orbit

as I perceive it. She and I are moving
at different speeds. Time slows down the faster

I go. Imagine a scene, I'm holding
the most precious thing, and in this nowhen,

I'm not running, not free-falling.
I'm standing right where I always wanted

to be, farther from the dying days
of distant stars. Imagine a scene,

forces of nature weakening
in a universe that's expanding faster

perhaps than even light can traverse it.
Somewhere the future is happening,

a wrinkle—fickle and unfolding.
My heart, from beat to beat, knows only

that I am holding the most precious thing.
Time speeds up as I imagine this scene.

IN THE ISLAND OF GOOD BOOTS

> *"One had to be groomed—by culture, by tradition, by authority—into servitude."*
> —Ninotchka Rosca

Of course, *kasama*
sounds gentler, more
charitable, somehow, less
demeaning, even, when
compared to *katulong*,
utusán or—heaven
forbid—*alipin*
(a word which hasn't been used
in over five decades).

Kikay/Emmy/Malou/Lourdes/
Betty/Alice/Gigi/Baby/
Fracing/Honey/Anali/Ming/
Puring/Nora/Lilia/Yaya/
Manang—
Pakibili ako ng _____.
Pakikuha yung _____.
Paki plantsa.

Paki- is a gentler—somehow more
charitable, somehow less
demeaning—version of *utos*.

One had to be groomed—
by culture, by tradition,
by station—
to be a benevolent master.
Pakitali—
Please tie my shoes.

FALSE MEMORY

Paper-like bracts
of bougainvillea, pink
and high-strung, clung
to the walls of the villa
the morning my great-
grandmother polished
her floors with coconut
husk until they shone.

She made sweet sticky
rice cake and curdled
coconut cream to go
with it. And before
she expired, she roasted
six cups of rice until
almost the color of sorrow,
steeped the toasty grains
in hot water, her version
of coffee for the guests

her daughters did not know
were coming. She was dead
by evening, her blood
already too thick
for tension. It was odd
how she knew this, the same way

she knew her faithless
husband would drop
dead after she willed it.
There is so much more
to the story, but I'll stop
with the flowers,
and how they bled me.
How warlike they can be.

THE ART OF SALAMAT

"Taos pusong pasasalamat"
(*Gracias, desde lo*
más profundo de mi corazón)
must then be prepositional
for it invokes the heart,
once believed to be the seat
of all affective states
of consciousness. To thank
deeply and sincerely
(that is, heartfully
and prepositionally) implies
that there is a recipient,
a benefactor, and a good deed done.
(Very different from propositional
gratitude, which merely suggests
a recipient's appreciation
for a general state of affairs,
such as freedom from want,
or the absence of rain
on any given day.)
To thank someone in Filipino
is to say, "*Salamat*" (most likely
Arabic in origin, for the Arabs
frequented a precolonial
Philippines via ancient trade routes).
To use the Filipino's language

of gratitude is to carry
the heft of a sacred duty.
For every Filipino is aware
that "*utang na loob*" is a debt
that can never be entirely,
truly settled. This means,
the beneficiary is also,
in equal measure, trustee—
keeper of the obligations
of gratitude, and honorable
enough to repay a favor.
In other words, *marunong
tumanaw ng utang na loob.*
Whether every act
of beneficence calls
for some degree of goodwill
is debatable. "After 337
days holding out against soldiers
of the Katipunan, the small
Spanish detachment (barricaded
inside Baler's fortress-like church)
finally surrendered. In an act
of benevolence, President Aguinaldo,
in eighteen ninety nine, decreed
that 'the survivors shall be treated
as friends not as prisoners.'"
100 years later, in an equally
"momentous gesture, Spain's Congreso
de Diputados formally expressed

their country's gratitude
toward the Philippines
for declaring the Philippine-Spanish
Friendship Day on June 30
of every year in commemoration
of the historic Siege of Baler.
Spain's unprecedented move
was made in response
to an equally unprecedented
initiative by the Philippines
to pass Republic Act 9187..."
For this and other acts
of beneficence, descendants
of the Spanish soldiers
continue to bespeak gestures
of goodwill—like the Philippine flag
flying in perpetuity
in someone's ancestral home
somewhere on the Iberian
peninsula. Or snatches
of *lengua castellano*
afloat some island
on the Philippine
archipelago. Some days,
gratitude is a canvas
funnel that restrains movement;
it may also be that it is all
that prevents you from drifting
too far too soon.

MARTIAL LAW BABIES

Ask me what it means to be island-bred
I will tell you how we used to travel

For hours on a bus to feel sand
Beneath us, pinked with bodies of dead

Coral and mollusk, traces of saltwater
Oyster. How unfancy we were, making

Bubbles from pink hibiscus flowers.
How the other best part of the day was

Sweetest pink shaved ice topped with milk powder.
Monsooned and gorged, we always meant to give

More than we took. But I don't speak for everyone.
I am someday and halfway, tell me

How to return to you unyearned
On a bus, unfettered, pink-lanterned.

BALIKBAYAN

Ocean-born, I was always bound
to come home to a sea
that has no memory
of me, save for my stars,
long-lived and feather-like.
Bayan kong binabalik-balikan

so close to the coastline,
I hear sounds as they move
just above the water's surface,
the rare glide upward,
the slide and swing, the extra note.
Bayan kong binabalik-balikan

I hear your heartbeat
this far from your shore.
What we saved at the water's edge,
we also left behind,
had hoped to endure—cone shells,
red corallines, O love of mine.

TO WANT THE WIDE AMERICAN EARTH

After Carlos Bulosan

In my mouth is a country of longing
The bittersweet of border crossings
Some words don't come easy—scarce, scars
English is a language of leaving
a lexicon of who invaded
and what they left behind. I taste
what passes for shrimp paste, crave spice,
some sharpness and haste. First train leaves
before first light, the last one before
midnight. Transport me with the sight
of filtered light. In my mouth is a country
of bittersweet crossings. Say *namamahay*
in English in the only space I will
ever occupy: this expanse of longing.

PAGBABALIK

My father returned twice to the river
now steeper than when he first knew it,
its wild waters meandering with the
widest bends. So much of who he was
was shaped by movement outside my line
of sight. So much struggle upriver before
reaching gravel and calmer waters.
My ancestors, the river dwellers, were known
in the history of Song to trade silk-
cotton for caldrons and betel nuts
for iron pots. But so much of how they lived
depended on mangroves and women
warriors who read Kawi and Sanskrit ciphers,
scripts on copper, the bluest star cluster.

LEGACY

To tell her story, you must know when
to put courage in a matchbox and conceal

it in a loaf of bread. You must learn how
a message betokened deliverance

when courage is simply a word someone
wrote on a slip of paper and the sweet

scent of bread could no longer sustain you.
You must grasp your other hand with what

grit remains, growing and unyielding.
To tell her story, you must walk in her shoes.

If forced out of your leased farmland,
don't forget to bring rice if you can pack

only what you can carry. And if
your mother did not speak inside the bus

with the windows covered with brown paper
on the way to the barracks, it was only

because she was praying that you would not be
housed in the horse stall with the manure

whitewashed over. And if you were, she was
deciding what to do about the smell.

To tell her story, you must remember
the landscape from behind barbed

wire fences. You must gaze at your body
and know its history, look beneath

the tender, ridged scars and see the bone
protruding out of your right arm

and hole the size of a football
on your right thigh, wondering how

the lights never went out. You must
look at the image of your grandmother

with the weight of rammed earth against
what you survived. To tell her story,

you must say a prayer, not of sorrow,
but of grace. You must loosen the earth,

pick daffodils to the base of the stem,
remember your roots and ordinary days,

and the grit under your fingernails,
the way your grandmother taught you.

AT THE CONVALESCENT HOME
FOR WINTER PLUMS,

      the sickest trees rarely survive
    the season. Too wounded
            and misshapen
    with monstrous knots
        around dead limbs,
              they perish
      steadily.
    In some, the girdled arms
              have grown sideways
      as though despairingly,
           and in perpetuity,

reaching for the sun.

DUST

Sometimes, we're like monsoon
winds, shifting east of where home is.
Sometimes, we're like tea leaves,

heavenly
and unfurling in agony.
This is how we shape

the earth. Dust up the Springs
and Autumns. See where it rained.
Which map bore our shade,

and which palace
to place above us, where our
majesty raised a dust.

A SHORT HISTORY OF JOURNEY

The fault, dear Arcturus, is not in your star.
I'm afraid we misread the swells
like explorers mistaking one continent for another.

"Columbus stretched out Asia eastward until Japan almost
    kissed the Azores."
"The Chinese treasure fleet had been mothballed long before
    Magellan set to sea."

In other words, they were imprecise, and they perished.

(Behold the flight of birds on rarefied air,
from breeding ground to wintering ground.
Behold intention, and its kin, precision.)

Be that as it may, we were always meant for motion.

See how the Silk Road was paved with horses' bones.
And more than smuggled silkworm, it brought sugar, silver,
paper—utter world changer.

See how the Spice Trade flourished,
shoring up an empire, its galleons—implacable bearers of a slave
trade from Manila to Acapulco.

The world got its cinnamon, its cocoa, its cassia
    and cardamom,
its lapis lazuli, and its Balas Ruby—ancient
    and sapphire-veined.
We got wanderlust.

And the bravest of us looked up and remembered everything—
the fixed star, the dippers, the king, the queen, the bear-keeper—
rubescent and fourth brightest in all the night sky, dearest,

remembered also the cardinal of old fields and every roadside—
brilliantly blue and sometimes true—in the same night sky,
roaming its way home.

AN AMERICAN SENTENCE

She's a newborn century so I told her to make a memory.

LONGITUDES

"Geography does not define you, love does."
—Eve Ensler

AN IMMIGRANT'S GUIDE TO NAVIGATING BORDERS AND BODIES OF WATER

1.

Save me a fish scale, hard tissue
and enamel, true cartographer.
Teach me how to unchart this body
of saltwater. Let me start over.
Between us is only skin and no other
border. Only salt and this still bone matter.
There are no monsters save the ones
we've slain when we were younger. O ocean,
O forebear, remember our blood and scar,
the ashes of our father. What we buried,
what we scattered at the edge of our future.
Wind and current, be witness, be sister,
augured and mothered, as we inch closer,
start over as we break these barriers.

2.

Start with fish scales and a fistful of ash.
O ancestor. O voyager. Here
is a prayer. All my life I've been moving
ever closer to the sea. But the maps
were wrong and nothing was where I thought
it would be. I need no chart this time.

Beneath me are lumber worth two thousand
teaks, a cargo of porcelain and silk,
sunk to lay claim to land and tidewater.
These were the monsters you've slain
when you were younger. Winged feet,
swim to the surface with feeding
hatchetfish. With my breastbone,
my backbone, my hearthstone.

3.

Salt and bone, I am ocean and uncharted.
I remember everything that was buried
and scattered. Augur and future. Be witness,
be braver, after I break these barriers.
Save me a fish scale, slayer of monsters.
On my life, I am inching closer
to the surface, winged feet and blister.
Beneath me are fleets, sunken
and surrendered. O forebear. O explorer.
The largest migration happens everyday
from deep ocean layers. I, too, have learned
to shift currents. My edge and center,
here is a prayer. Remember who you are.
Spine and shimmer, mover of water.

SPEAK POETRY

For my mom

I was taught to gather
Only what belonged to me
To never pick wildflowers
But instead commit
To memory the shape
And sound of what they
Shelter, painted lady
Bumblebee, when I say
Speak poetry—
I mean know the language
Of wild and fragile things
Speak of flight and firelight
How to measure a wingspan
A lifespan, a split second
That changes everything
Carry each other
The poet says, this matters
More than anything

WHAT I KNOW ABOUT JAWNS I LEARNED FROM ALLEN IVERSON

That crossover is a lot like a turn
you never see coming, be unguardable

like everything is poetry,
like the time Live 8 came to my city

(and I say my city though I was
practically FOB and knew

little of the jawns of a new country,
but Philly in July was a glory

of flowers, summersweet and spicy,
walked me through the biggest human heart

as though my own were not yet rivered
and wrung), threw a block party

outside my place on the Parkway
where Destiny's Child—my stars—and Black Ice

took me to church though I was a straight up
churchgoer (walked a mile every Sunday

to 17th & Chestnut, but not before
grabbing my coffee at Wawa's,

and just because I could, I would walk past
18th & Walnut where the *American*

Poetry Review was, not that I had the guts
to hand them my work), tell me again how to

walk through a human heart without
wearing it down, steal away to church

boots on the ground, watch that split second
where Iverson takes pen and paper,

draws you, straight up buries you, Blood,
he says, throw up a prayer, or walk.

HAINT BLUE

To free yourself of the haint,
you need to vanquish it.
Paint your porch
the color of water
which is power,
with the might to scatter
blue light to the green
of seawater. But remember
how heavy color can be.
How shades of blue
came from true indigo,
which needed an abundance
of water and limestone
above the bedrock before
it became a cash crop,
which needed to be pounded
and crushed, and dusted
with wood ash to make
blue cakes, which was the currency
of slavery: a bolt of cloth
dyed indigo for one human body.
But mixed with lime and some
white mineral, it resembled water
which haints could not cross over.

THERE ARE NO KINGS IN AMERICA

There are no kings in America,
we are not that kind of country.
We are sanctuary for the hungry,
the homeless, the huddled,
held together by an idea
our immigrant fathers believed in.
Rendered, it meant independence.
Pursued, it kindled war, ordnance,
a fighting chance. Forty thousand
musket balls, by themselves, did not
shape the boundaries on which we
map our days. To draw our borders,
we needed more than firecakes.
More than a pound of meat
with bone and gristle,
or salt fish and a gill of peas.
We needed the faith and grit of people
who were not yet Americans.
To be an American
is to recognize the sacrifice
of the widow and the orphan;
it is to understand the weft of tent
cities expecting caravans,
and the heft of a child in a camp
not meant for children, or sitting
before a judge awaiting judgement.

What do we say to the native
whose lands we now inhabit?
What do we say to our immigrant
fathers who held certain truths
to be self-evident?
Do we now still pledge to each
other our lives, our fortunes,
our sacred honor.
There are no kings in America.
Only gilded men we can topple
again and again.

TO TREASURE ISLAND FOR A WARDROBE FITTING BEFORE THE FUNERAL CORTÈGE IN SEASON 4 OF MAN IN THE HIGH CASTLE

With a line by Philip K. Dick

    I had no lines, but got along
with the costume designer who dressed
me as an officer's wife and decided
I should wear the vintage black tulle
and satin whimsy hat perhaps to make
up for the black pumps that were not
designed for comfort, and since I was
a background actor in an alternate
history, what was the harm in unlearning
who won which war as long as
my grandmother didn't turn in her grave
because I don't think she ever got over
what she had to do in the years before
liberation. Looking in the mirror

        in a retro skirt suit, I thought I saw
a ghost. But it is twenty eighteen
in the real world, and Treasure Island
is a boneyard, a place for old longings
where the only ghosts are long-gone lady
beetles and irradiated moths. Steel
shipping containers sit atop the bones

of a walled city, and there's a white
retriever with a six-pound lump
on his belly and the sight of him,
I know, will forever haunt me.
Here we are where the World's Fair was,
and I wonder what we were before
we were this, quarried rock that bloomed

      into something more radioactive.
Before we could walk towards something
terrible or divine (in the last
hour before sunset and after
many resets)—pretend mourners
behind the opulent palanquin
in our retro modern black skirt suits
and veiled black hats and the almost
unbearable classic black shoes—
we had a wardrobe fitting, took off
our clothes and looked in the mirror,
saw an island rising, or a murmuration,
starlings gathering into something
terrible, or something divine.

THE OLDEST ENGLISH-SPEAKING SETTLEMENT ON THE SAN FRANCISCO PENINSULA

in winter, beyond
the walled garden and the frost-
dusted yew, quince

STILL, LIKE AIR

we rise toward
      the light, our movement
           widening as though

in prayer, holy
      and urgent. I will
           say your name—

an act of love
      more powerful than
           the weight of air

or the falling of light.
      Like clouds speaking
           their truth—every

heap and layer, every
      curl of hair, a reckoning.
           Still, I pray

for grace, to hear
      your story, and what
           you know of clouds—

why they shine
      at night, where they
           touch the ground,

how they birth a star.
      Perhaps you will
           want to know

my story, and why these
      queries—like, what
           will it cost

to cross an inch
      of scorn? Or climb a wall
           of fear? How much

to plough the air,
      to read the clouds?
           How much for a sip

of water, a gulp
      of air? How much
           for three square

feet of space?
      For the narrowest
           breathing place?

How much for
      the life of my child.
           Still, I ask—

an act
      of grace as I rise
           toward the light.

HOW TO BUILD A LIFE

> *"all you need is flour, water, and a little bit of time"*
> —The Public Science Lab

We named her Pony beebalm after the flower.
Fed her twice a day at first with flour
and water, how she rose and rose, fierce
and free-living, how this moment and that fit
together the first year we sheltered.
We cared wildly that the splendid poison
frog will no longer be calling. The sour-
dough was too dense, but we ate our mistakes
anyway. Sent meals to the local hospital,
but the body collectors kept coming
anyway. All that love, rammed and buried.
We could not make sense of it. So we grew
tomatoes, beans, bee balms. Fed our incautious
dreams. We loved to the bone, and kept walking.

KISS ME OVER THE GARDEN GATE

find me a forgotten footpath,
meet me by Water Dog Lake.
Wooded cleft and waterbody
startle me with starthistle
and Christmas berry, holly-
like and evergreen cherry.
Let me tarry, tiger salamander.
There's something I wished to find.
From the gathered seedhead that grew
the heirloom bloom, a heart-shaped
leaf, the life and pith and journey with.

AI IS LOVE

and deep as midnight
the way Arun
is the color of first light—
a fiery vein into
cotton ball clouds.

In San Francisco when the air
is salty and fair,
love is him—a bowl lute,
harplike and earnest.
And it is her, dark tresses
and long white dress.

On the Malabar Coast,
love is monsoon and sun glitter.
In the land where the sun rises,
it is a thousand paper cranes,
squash-folded and golden.

Here is a wish and the wish is love.
And love is a promise,
and the promise is hers.
In her long white dress,
she is everything. Every sunrise
and a thousand paper cranes.

TREE LIGHTING AT FREMONT PARK IN THE SECOND YEAR OF THE PANDEMIC

May we ever constellate around each other.
Like a blessing, a season of giving.
May we bear witness to moments that bring
waxwing closer to mistletoe berry,
wintering sparrow to crabapple and bramble.
More of this and each other, of giving thanks for
the evergreen oak, acorn-bearer and emblem
of power. Of honoring the Ohlone
who relied on the oak tree, and ground acorns
into a meal, and gifted each other
their finest flour. As we constellate, may we
find sweetness in what we've dried and roasted,
chestnuts, figs. From my hand to yours, and yours
to mine, these grains, like a prayer for winter.

POETRY, PLEASE

And when we speak let it be said
that nothing is lost in translation.

That our words are true and tenable.
That we understand the meaning of "sii,"

the Ohlone word for water, which is you.
The Ohlone knew this. They were first

of this county, borne of seawater
and woven reeds to salt marshes

and pickleweeds and saltwater silvered
by smelt. They fared on abalone

and blue elderberry. Western
chokecherry. Periwinkle. Oaks.

All flourishing, grace-filled, transitory.
If I were a weaver, I would gift you

a basket made of sandbar willow
and tule, bright as cinnabar.

But I can only write this poem,
a tributary, to carry

the weight of water as it flows
and hefts the meaning of you.

Giver and taker.
And everything that I knew.

HERE BE DRAGONS, CETACEANS, PINK CRUSTACEANS, DEAR HUMANS & A BOOK OF REMEMBRANCE

The cavalry's here,
loud as thunder, wild and wiser,
like a nobility
of beasts—catch the light
where x marks the spot
and if anyone asks,
this poem is a map
that lapses daily,
sees clearly two seadragons
spinning snout-to-snout
and pods of cetaceans
fueled by clouds
of pink crustaceans—
the shape of the Arctic
is less solid now,
fading into swaths
of milky blue—
and above us, dying stars
consuming their weight
in gas and dust—we're a throbbing
mass of grief and limbs
like whale food, or swollen
coastlines—do me a kindness
and repeat this worship

of humans, their book
of remembrance
a cadence of heartbeats
more than a thousand
a minute, short-winged
and foraging for flowers
which bloomed much earlier.
If I could I would
gather this shimmer—
this wonder of stars,
stop the world from burning,
the seas from rising—
be the cavalry
or a reliance of stewards:
remember what it means to love you

A TRADE WAR IN FULL BLOOM, OR HOW TO UNPACK THE LOVE LANGUAGE OF PERISHABLES AS IMPORT DUTIES WILT THE FRAGILE TRADE OF FLOWERS

A Hay(na)ku

Tariff
cut roses,
disrupt love unseasonably

TAKE HEART

Take heart from a hummingbird, a handful
of earth. See how memory bears fruit,
to carry history, healing, offspring.
Listen for sounds gently rising above
the hum and din, the prayers of one so far
from home and kin. Say you remembered
to put out feeders, withhold water
from inflorescent tomcat clovers.
Say you are here in lieu of flowers.
What did you lose the year of our
sheltering. Whom do you honor with
the hope you bring. Take heart, listen, sounds
of kindness are bouncing off hard surfaces.
Praise bedside care and all its auspices.

FIREBORN

I once went wild
over repurposed things—
tweeds, beads, driftwood, silvery
wormwood got worked
into frames, footgear, chandeliers.
My favorite, though,
is a floor lamp from a limb
trimmed from an old manzanita,
the color of burnished red pear.
Wild child of the last wildfire,
evergreen and unsparing,
our gratitude for the little apples,
and the many equally
wild and resolute things
that fed on them—
that charm of hummingbirds,
that grist of bees,
that flutter of butterflies.
You were the kindling,
and the offering,
the timeworn prayer
above the movement of air.

FIELD NOTES FROM COOLEY LANDING

On Puichon land, between open water
and shoreline, the tidal marshes are coming
back—by every measure a miracle
since time and settler had reworked it
into a brownfield, a dump site where things go
for burning. What breathes now, between marsh
and mudflat, are forage and shelter—
saltbush, gumplant, shimmery saltgrass.
On any map, you can hardly see
what the red lines had done to us, what had been
buried in concrete now lies with the wetlands.
The salt marsh harvest mouse, button-eyed
and a little bigger than my thumb,
is a mischief in a patch of pickleweed.

CATALOG OF CURES IN ORDINARY TIME

There's a prayer for every malady
    in ordinary time if you know where to look,
said my father, and though he kept his daily
    devotions and entreaties to himself, I found
a psalter in his pocket the final summer
    he rescued clusters of sungold tomatoes
from early blight. Like little sunsets, like a song
    of ascents, I wish to remember my father.
Not my recollections of blossoms and blossom-end rot
    which are fading evenly, but the whole
inventory of days when my father picked
    early corn in late August, milk stage of kernels,
brown silks for corn silk tea that was meant to be
    anti-inflammatory. In the end,
it was fast and metastatic, and I've learned
    that what grows from seed to seed is a lesson

in acceptance. What was fallow ground, for instance,
    has been broken up. Here lie the barkflies and the dead moths
and aphids, repelled by my summer savory—
    beloved of honeybees, peppery
and a good remedy for too salty
    recipes—also sweet costmary, green
and silvery (but remember to use
    sparingly). Lemon balm, in remembrance of my father,
is the hardiest and longest-lived of them

    all, growing back each year with a resolve
that is rigid and almost a respite
    from the grief that is lodged in the split between my heartbeats.

IN HALF MOON BAY

there are all these halves at the edge of the sea,
like half a heart of shore briefly cradling
a sea star that has bravely lost its arms.
When its stone coral mouth is already
drained of sea water, its spine of honeycombed
lime would be the last to go. At low tide,
the feisty and starry flounder leaves tracks
in pursuit of ghost shrimp; while the shy
and snowy plover wades in and out of waves,
not playing but foraging for sand hoppers,
its fortune tied with the tides like sand
and moonshine. But count on the bread to still
rise on century-old bricks six days a week,
like goodwill, or good fortune inside a wave.

GREAT EXPECTATIONS AT RACE & AUZERAIS

After Maya Angelou & Rebecca M. Archer

It is sunrise, with hope its arrogant/ rider. How it sprang up, buoyed,/ as I ran to catch the bus and almost/ missed it. There's a heartbeat in my throat./ Pretend I'm a rain bird or a fire horse/ fueled by miracles. I'm here/ short-winded and salted trying to catch/ my breath standing near the front of the bus/ gripping a handhold that is too high/ for me. I am radiant and impossible,/ and there's a bird caged in my throat, a poem/ in my pocket that aches to gallop, let go/ the handhold. Pretend I'm a versicle,/ a miracle, the hope that gets you going.

GLOSSARY

alipin	slave
balikbayan	a Filipino returning to the homeland
bayan kong binabalik-balikan	my homeland to which I return again and again
dinuguan	savory stew made from pork and pig's blood
hay naku	Oh my! / adapted into the hay(na)ku, a Filipino haiku variant by Eileen R. Tabios
kasama	companion
Katipunan	a revolutionary group founded in 1892 by Filipino nationalists
katulong	helper
lengua castellano	Spanish language
manang	a respectful way to address an older woman
marunong tumanaw ng utang na loob	knows how to repay a debt of gratitude
namamahay	feeling of unease in an unfamiliar place
pagbabalik	return
paki–	prefix that transforms a verb into a polite request

paki-plantsa	please iron [this]
pakibili ako ng _____	please buy me _____
pakikuha yung _____	please go get _____
pakitali	please tie [this]
salamat	thank you
sinta	beloved
taos pusong pasasalamat / gracias, desde lo más profundo de mi corazón	heartfelt thanks
utang na loob	debt of gratitude
utos	command
utusán	servant

MAPPING MIGRATIONS:
A PERSONAL & INCOMPLETE HISTORY

2000 BC: Rice cultivation in the Philippines

1300s: Pre-colonial adoption of the Baybayin script

1521: Ferdinand Magellan, leading the 1519–1522 Spanish expedition to the East Indies, arrives in the Philippines

1565: The Philippines falls under New Spain's colonial administration; the Manila–Acapulco Galleon Trade route opens, linking Asia and the Americas

1587: Filipino sailors arrive in what is now Morro Bay, California aboard the Spanish galleon *Nuestra Señora de Buena Esperanza*

1593: Publication of the *Doctrina Christiana*, first printed book in the Philippines

1611: Spanish Dominican missionaries establish the University of Santo Tomas, the oldest existing university in Asia

1762-1764: British occupation of Manila

1763: First recorded Filipino settlement in the U.S. in Saint Malo, Louisiana

1896-1898: Philippine Revolution against Spain

1898: Filipino revolutionaries declare Philippine independence

1898: The United States defeats Spain at the Battle of Manila Bay

1898: Spain cedes the Philippines to the United States under the Treaty of Paris, establishing the first U.S. colony

1899-1902: Philippine-American War

1901: Centralized public education system modeled after the U.S. system begins with English as medium of instruction

1902: The Philippine-American War officially ends, reinforcing the shift to U.S. civil rule established the previous year

1903: First U.S.-sponsored Filipino scholars (*pensionados*) arrive to study in American colleges

1905: Author's maternal great-grandfather moves to the U.S.

1906: First Filipino laborers migrate to the U.S. to work in Hawaiian plantations, West Coast farms, lumber camps, and Alaska canneries (second wave of Filipino immigration to the U.S.; Filipinos being U.S. nationals were permitted entry but restricted citizenship rights)

1920s-1930s: Anti-Filipino riots and enforcement of anti-miscegenation laws against Filipinos in the U.S.

1925: Publication of the first book of poetry in English by a Filipino author (G.P. Putnam's Sons, New York: *Azucena* by Mariano de Gracia Concepción)

1930s-1950s: Philippines as Jazz Capital of Asia

1935: Philippine Constitution designates English, alongside Spanish, as an official language of the Philippines

1942-1945: Japan occupies the Philippines during the Second World War

1945: End of Japanese occupation

1946: The United States recognizes Philippine Independence under the Treaty of Manila

1946: Publication of *America Is in the Heart* by Carlos Bulosan, often regarded as the father of Filipino American literature

1946-1960s: Third wave of Filipino immigration to the U.S. (veterans, nurses, and other professionals)

1949: Jose Garcia Villa introduces his "comma poems" merging Filipino American identity with modernist poetic form

1965-1970: Delano Grape Strike (landmark labor movement with significant Filipino American involvement)

1965-present: Filipino professional migration and family reunification (fourth wave of Filipino immigration to the U.S.)

1972-1981: Martial Law in the Philippines

1970s-2000: Four generations of the author's family establish roots in California

1994: Founding of Philippine American Women Writers and Artists (PAWWA) which reorganizes as Philippine American Writers and Artists, Inc. (PAWA) in 1998

2000: Author settles in the U.S.

2001-2016: *Our Own Voice*, one of the earliest Filipino American online literary journals, edited by Remé-Antonia Grefalda (founding curator of the Asian and Pacific Islander Collection at the Library of Congress), in publication

2003: Eileen R. Tabios invents the hay(na)ku poetic form

2004: Release of *Pinoy Poetics: A Collection of Autobiographical and Critical Essays on Filipino and Filipino American Poetics*, published by Eileen R. Tabios and edited by Nick Carbó

2009: U.S. Congress officially recognizes October as Filipino American History Month

2016: Founding of Paloma Press, first Filipino American/ Southeast Asian publisher on the San Francisco Peninsula

2023: Release of *Dear Human at the Edge of Time: Poems on Climate Change in the United States* as a companion to the congressionally mandated Fifth National Climate Assessment (NCA5), with Luisa A. Igloria as lead editor, published by Paloma Press

2025: *Wanna Peek Into My Notebook?: Notes on Pinay Liminality* by Barbara Jane Reyes, published by Paloma Press in 2022, wins the Best Book Award from the Filipino Studies Section of the Association for Asian American Studies

2025: Release of *The Nature of Our Times: Poems on America's Lands, Waters, Wildlife, and Other Natural Wonders* as a Poets for Science anthology and companion to the first national assessment of U.S. lands, waters, and wildlife, with Luisa A. Igloria as lead editor, published by Paloma Press in partnership with Wick Poetry Center at Kent State University and United By Nature

---

References:

Annals of Botany
Filipinas Heritage Library
Filipino American National Historical Society Journal
Library of Congress Research Guides
Office of the Historian (U.S.)
Stanford Medicine Ethnogeriatrics
U.S. Department of Labor

ACKNOWLEDGMENTS

"Let Me Call You Sweetheart," originally commissioned for ManifestDifferently.org, first appeared in *Consequence* 16.2, October 2024. Quotes from "Dewey at Manila Bay—Lessons in Operational Art and Operational Leadership from America's First Fleet Admiral" by Derek B. Grange, *Naval War College Review*, vol. 64, no. 4, 2011, article 10, and "President McKinley Puts the Philippines on the U.S. Map," SHEC: *Resources for Teachers*.

"Traje de Boda" first appeared in *Traje de Boda* (Meritage Press, 2009).

"Heritage Fruit" first appeared in *Santelmo* (Issue 4, March 2023).

"I Am, Villanelle" first appeared in *The Bloom*, March 2022.

"Viand" first appeared in *Traje de Boda* (Meritage Press, 2009).

"Orange Jessamine Road" first appeared in *Our Own Voice*, April 2012.

"Imagine" was awarded 2nd place in the Inaugural Brilliant Poetry Prize (2024).

"In the Island of Good Boots" first appeared in *Galatea Resurrects* (2017) in response to Alex Tizon's article, "My Family Slave" (*The Atlantic*, June 2017).

"False Memory" first appeared in *Santelmo* (Issue 4, March 2023).

The Art of Salamat was published by Moria Poetry as part of the Locofo Chaps project (2017). Quotes from "Spain Proclaims Gratitude for Philippines' Friendship in Historic Parliamentary Declaration," Senate of the Philippines, 20th Congress, 8 July 2011.

"Martial Law Babies" appeared in *100 Pink Poems Para Kay Leni*, edited by Krip Yuson et al (San Anselmo Publications, 2022) and *Cultural Daily* (September 2022).

"Balikbayan" was adapted from "Tanaga: After Katy de la Cruz" (*Poetry*, July/August 2021); it was set to music by composer Saunder Choi and premiered at the Pasadena Conservatory of Music in 2024.

"To Want the Wide American Earth" was commissioned and set to music by composer Saunder Choi for the National Masterwork Chorus & Orchestra's "A New Beginning" which premiered at Carnegie Hall in 2023.

"Pagbabalik" first appeared in *Marías at Sampaguitas* (Issue 3, December 2021)

"Legacy" appeared in *Marsh Hawk Press Review* (Spring 2021) and poets.org.

"At the Convalescent Home for Winter Plums," first appeared in *Moria Poetry* (Fall 2010/Winter 2011).

"Dust" was commissioned for the 10th Annual CSM Asian Pacific American Film Festival at the College of San Mateo (2019); an audio recording was also aired on KALW Public Radio in January 2023.

"A Short History of Journey" appeared in San Francisco Public Library's Poem of the Day curated by San Francisco Poet Laureate Kim Shuck (May 2020) and in poets.org. Quotes from *Admiral of the Ocean Sea* by Samuel Eliot Morison (Little, Brown and Company, 1991), cited in *IEEE Spectrum*, 2012, and *Over the Edge of the World* by Laurence Bergreen (MJF Books, 2015), cited in *CNN*, 2003.

"An American Sentence" was written as part of the Postcard Project (2025) curated by Eileen R. Tabios.

"An Immigrant's Guide to Navigating Borders and Bodies of Water" first appeared in *West Trestle Review* (November/December 2023). It was originally commissioned for Metro Film and Arts' "Breaking Down Walls" (2022) production.

"Speak Poetry" appeared in *American Poets* (Fall/Winter 2022) and as part of "The Laureate Fellows' Collaborative Poem" in poets.org.

"What I Know About Jawns I Learned From Allen Iverson" first appeared in *Mount Hope Magazine* (October 2024).

"Haint Blue" appeared in the *San Francisco Chronicle* (June 2020) and poets.org.

"There are no kings in America" was first read at the San Mateo County Board of Supervisors Meeting in July 2019, and has since appeared in print and in other adaptations in *Vox Populi* (2020), the Academy of American Poets (2022), the U.S. Consulate General in Shanghai (2022), the Poetry Foundation (2023), Poetry Out Loud (2023), and the 250th anniversary of the American Revolution in Concord, Massachusetts (2025).

"To Treasure Island for a wardrobe fitting before the funeral cortège in Season 4 of Man in the High Castle" first appeared in *Mount Hope Magazine* (October 2024).

"The Oldest English-Speaking Settlement on the San Francisco Peninsula" was written to inaugurate Filoli's Annual Haiku Competition (2020).

"Still, Like Air" first appeared in *Positively Filipino* (February 2019).

"How to Build a Life" first appeared in *Santelmo* (Issue 4, March 2023).

"Kiss Me Over the Garden Gate" was one of several poetry installations in Belmont commissioned in 2019 and 2020 by then poet laureate Jacki Rigoni.

"Ai Is Love" first appeared in *G U E S T* edited by Melissa Eleftherion (2021).

"Tree Lighting at Fremont Park in the Second Year of the Pandemic" was commissioned by Menlo Park Library for the city's 2021 Tree Lighting Ceremony. It appeared in *The Poetry Lighthouse* in January 2024.

"Poetry, please" was the author's inaugural poem as Poet Laureate of San Mateo County (2019).

"Here be dragons, cetaceans, pink crustaceans, dear humans & a book of remembrance" appeared in *Dear Human at the Edge of Time* (2023) and *Anthropocene* (January 2024).

"A Trade War in Full Bloom, or How to Unpack the Love Language of Perishables as Import Duties Wilt the Fragile Trade of Flowers" first appeared in the *St. Helena Star* (May 2025) as part of Eileen R. Tabios' regular poetry column.

"Take Heart" was commissioned as part of the 2022 Commemoration Events for San Mateo County Healthcare Workers. It appeared in the *San Francisco Chronicle*, *Half Moon Bay Review*, and *Pacifica Tribune* in 2022.

"Fireborn" appeared in *California Fire & Water: A Climate Crisis Anthology* edited by Nevada County Poet Laureate Molly Fisk (2020), and was presented as part of the 2020 Genoa International Poetry Festival.

"Field Notes from Cooley Landing" first appeared in *Rust & Moth* (August 2024).

"Catalog of Cures in Ordinary Time" won the 2025 Foley Poetry Prize and first appeared in *America Magazine* (June 2025).

"In Half Moon Bay" first appeared in *The Banyan Review* (Spring 2020).

"Great Expectations at Race & Auzerais" was part of an ekphrastic collaboration with artist Rebecca M. Archer, and also appeared in Sims Library of Poetry's Poem-a-Week (November 2023). First line from *Shaker, Why Don't You Sing?* by Maya Angelou (Random House, 1983).

With heartfelt thanks to everyone who made room for these journeys, and my husband and family who made it all worthwhile.

Photo by Paul Cassinetto

Aileen Cassinetto is a 2021 Academy of American Poets Laureate Fellow and winner of the 2025 Foley Poetry Prize. She is also a co-editor of *Dear Human at the Edge of Time: Poems on Climate Change in the United States* (2023), a companion to the congressionally mandated Fifth National Climate Assessment (NCA5), and *The Nature of Our Times: Poems on America's Lands, Waters, Wildlife, and Other Natural Wonders* (2025), a companion to United by Nature: A Knowledge Assessment of Nature and Nature's Benefits in the U.S. (formerly First U.S. National Nature Assessment or NNA1).

www.ingramcontent.com/pod-product-compliance
Lightning Source LLC
Chambersburg PA
CBHW060621080526
44585CB00013B/929